table of contents

1

destination

"Without a goal, there is nothing to shoot for."

We need to aim for something concrete and visible. Could you imagine a basketball game without a rim or net? Crazy for sure.

This holds true in your organization and your life, and the game of basketball as well.

So, we simply need to start this book by naming *it*. *It*.
It is your dream, the goal, the victory.

What are you trying to accomplish? Where are you and your team trying to go? What is the *destination*? There is something that your team needs to accomplish in the next 30 days, 3 months, or over the next year. It's good questions to answer for setting your *destination*.
DESTINATION (noun): *a desired common goal of where you will arrive as a team.*
Why? Why do you need to do something? It is important
as you need people to know and believe in the mission, the dream and the why.

Eggers, is the Founder and President of *LeaderShift Insights, Inc.* She has a simple, yet profound, model for us in this regard. It is called the

According to Eggers, there are 4 stages to the process of mobilizing people to drive action, together: clarify, focus, align, act.

Phase 2: FOCUS = Name and frame the opportunity

Phase 4: ACT = Determine solutions and execute A critical mistake many tend to make is we want to jump from seeing a problem (clarify) and leap directly into solutions (action). Action is important, but we need the *team* to accomplish and sustain results. Creating alignment with a team of people moving toward a common goal means that we involve them.

To reach your *destination* it will take everyone involved to bring it to fruition.
This is a great process for success.
You need to have a framework (clarity), a focus on the

your team to align around the fact that there is a problem they play a role in solving. This is critical to achieving a shared agenda.

Notice the word isn't *agree,* it is *align.* Have an
creating alignment with everyone. Once you have alignment, you can
develop solutions and your next step in setting your *destination.*
What & When…Where? Now is the time to create the detail of what you
will

need and the objective. Solutions, solutions, solutions! Brainstorm, be
creative, dive deep into how you can address your why. What you will do is
the catalyst to getting you to your *where.*

Keep in mind this truth. Teams that reach their destination do so together. So,
your destination needs to be a common goal, not just a goal. Align the team
on *why,* and then align and build a collaborative *what* as your detailed plan to
arrive.

You also need to state the timeframe of getting the work done. Without a
when, your work can drag along. Put a stake in the ground and pick a date.

"A goal is a dream with a deadline."
Napoleon Hill
We all love stories, so let's see this in action.

The late championship coach, Jim Valvano from North Carolina State
University men's basketball program, is such an inspiring example of
visually seeing

1978 team had one goal, win the national championship. They knew it would
take many elements to happen.
destination and having alignment with all participants.

Not only did they name it, Coach Valvano wrote down the goal on an index
card and carried it in his suit pocket. He knew that by clearly seeing the goal
(like cutting down a basketball net) written down and sharing with people for
accountability, their likelihood of succeeding increased. He knew then what
research has proven now.

Dr. Gail Matthews, a psychology professor at Dominican University in
California, recently completed

groups in the study was asked to think of a goal they wanted to accomplish. While another group was asked to

then build an action plan for success. In the end, the study concluded that workers who follow these simple steps are 42 percent more likely to achieve their goals when they

Now that's powerful!

Back to Coach Valvano and his team who were well on their way to victory. Beyond strategy, they took one more great step to *see* the destination.

the court with a ladder and a pair of scissors. They would take turns climbing the ladder and cutting down a piece of the net until the hoop was naked of any nylon.

Funny way to practice basketball, huh?

Not really when you think that there is just one team each year that wins the national championship. That team is the only team that gets to cut down the nets!

Coach Valvano and his team wanted to win. They worked the process, they wrote it down, they found accountability by sharing the dream with others and they made it real by visualizing the win!

Even though your situation isn't a game, it is actually much more important than that, you can use these principles to build your *destination*. As a team, with a well built action plan that is visualized by everyone, you *can* and *will* ignite your journey to success.

detailed in the closer time frames. You need more
objective due in 90 days versus one due in 3 years.

At this point, I have a strong suggestion for you, *stop reading*! Go get your team and *write it down*. Seriously, stop reading and work the above process with your team and write down the *destination*. You will most certainly be glad you did.

"All you need is the plan, the roadmap, and the courage to press on to your destination."

Earl Nightingale
My Destination

My Time Frame

How the Best Teams Win

2

evaluation

McCarver and Sons was a chain of hardware stores throughout the Midwest. It was founded in 1958 by its
over the last 56 years.

chain, Ace Hardware, McCarver and Sons was struggling to keep up and as a result, its 27 stores and 142 employees were facing immediate downsizing unless something was done.

Michael called in a sales and marketing expert, Russ Richards, to give him and his family an assessment of how to improve the company's portfolio. What Richards discovered was there had never been a serious

corporation. The reason? McCarver and Sons had made just enough money every year to survive and pay the family enough salary

Richards sat down with Michael and his family and gave them the hard news, "We need to do a serious evaluation of your assets, liabilities, sales techniques, product line and marketing strategies or you will not survive in the 21st Century."

The McCarver's were shocked. They had not expected such a harsh indictment of their beloved operation.

Richards began with the most basic change, "We need to give your company a new name, something that is contemporary and tells the public exactly what you sell. Your current name does not tell new customers what you're selling. I suggest a new brand name, *Hardware 4 You.*"

Michael McCarver immediately called for a recess, went into the bathroom and threw up. He was dramatically affected by the radical change that Richards was proposing.

When he returned, the family members and Richards spent the next three days intensely painfully evaluating every aspect of the company. Their process of evaluation led to new strategies, and new success.

they rose to number 3 in their markets. success. They were also to be commended for having the guts to bring in a marketing expert. They listened to that expert, believed in his ideas, and had the courage to execute them.

Every successful team understands the power of *evaluation*. Without taking the time to realistically assess the state of affairs in an organization, the future may not exist.

"Change before you have to."
Jack Welch, former CEO of General Electric
The main way that a future of success can be guaranteed is for the leader of an organization to swallow
or unpleasant, with genuine humility.
her image may color the view of the true *value* of the organization.
EVALUATION *(verb): to determine the*
by careful appraisal and study. One would think that every team would be in favor of constant evaluations, right?
In the inimitable words of Lee Corso,
"Not so fast my friend!"
Evaluations for organizations are hard to come by.
1. Resistance to change

Human nature hates change. Most of us would rather suffer with our status quo problems than face solving them. Teams are run by human beings. Change is painful. Evaluations may force the pain of change.

We see this in the simplest things in life. Most people sit in the same seats at church. They take the same routes in their commutes to work. They even tend to stop at the same coffee shop each morning. We are creatures of habit, and therefore, evaluation leads to changes which leads to pain.

2. Money

Evaluation costs money, and if implemented with changes, costs a lot *more* money. Groups, associations, organizations, school districts, are struggling would rather put whatever money they have into their pockets today, instead of into evaluations for tomorrow.

3. "What if we're wrong?"

not only was there a waste of effort and energy, but a waste of time and money too. So, a lot of people adhere to the policy, "Let sleeping dogs lie."

Again, we must be critical of ourselves.
We must ask tough questions.

You know what? You may be wrong.
But, what if you're right?

This isn't about taking crazy risks with disregard for prudent process. Rather, this is about under standing that fear will cripple you if you let it. Doing nothing new will keep you from doing every thing great.

4. Criticism

Whenever there is an evaluation, the team opens itself up to criticism by all stakeholders involved who suspected all along that something was

could result in a breakdown of morale. A leader who embraces *evaluation* is humble enough to admit he or she needs to reconsider their plan of attack in making their company more successful.

That is the kind of leader every organization needs to evolve and grow to heights never experienced before.

Here is a "classic" example of an evaluation disaster. Literally.
eroding and the CEO and his marketing team sat down and evaluated a possible solution to boost sales.

They decided to scrap their classic soft drink and came up with a product that would rival the Edsel as one of the most disastrous marketing campaigns in history.

We knew it as, "The New Coke."

They tried a "new" taste test with over 200,000 consumers and got a thumbs up. What Coke failed to realize was that their original soft drink was still beloved by all the customers out there, including the taste testers. They were approving a new product, not picking it over the one they grew up with.

The outcry over New Coke was so deafening that the company quickly retreated. A few months later there was no more New Coke, just the original one and the corporation survived.

The effect that marketing mistake had on the consumer market was tremendous. It made customers
thriving again.

So, in a manner of speaking, *evaluation* worked for the company, just not in the way they originally planned. By shaking up their cherished product and trying something new, it made the original more in demand.

Yet, they were smart of enough to *evaluate* again. Ironic, huh?
The same holds true for you, and me too.

Establishing and growing my business as a professional speaker has been about constant evaluation.

Very early on I met with a speaker who had over 45 years of experience. I sent him a manuscript for a book and the link to my brand new DIY website. I was so excited!

My new book, my thoughts, my heart for people; this was going to be awesome.
I really had reached out to ask him how to better launch my speaking career, get some speaking gigs, and

need you to give me the short version of your 45 year career. Well, he hated most everything.

He asked me, " are you serious about this business or just playingaround? This isn't a book, this is terrible! Nobody, and I mean nobody, willwant to read this!"

Ouch!
brutal truth hurt. I thought to myself, are you trying to help me or destroy me? Yet, notice the word used above, *truth*.
As I collected my thoughts the realization came over me; he was right.

I came to an experienced veteran for advice and as I listened I could see how wisdom and some evaluation would make the product and the brand better.

evaluation, what do you suggest?"

My friend Pat said, "Let's start over, I'll help you. You have tremendous concepts and plenty of material, we just need to present and package it in a manner that people will love. When you do that, they won't put the book down and they will book you! Trust me, you'll see."

I did. And we did. His advice made a huge impact!

We created a powerful brand, and FoxPoint was launched, and fast. As one speaking gig led to another, the books and video resources did as well.

Years later, I'm proud of the messages we deliver, and thankful for the clients that make our brand grow. I'm grateful for being humble enough to ask for help and truly evaluate what it takes to make it.

This story is just one example of how I continue to use *evaluation* in my business.

Every year I attend National Speaker Association meetings, read articles from experts and network with peers to learn, share and improve.

As I look into new products, markets and strategies, there are several successful speakers and business leaders I reach out to for ideas. Their input drives the ongoing process of *evaluation* for my company and brand.

I have developed a MasterMind Group that I reach out to either monthly or quarterly to brainstorm, collaborate and learn. See, the interaction of thought leaders actually helps each of us on our journey.

Here is the key point:

"To achieve real success, you need to be really honest in your evaluations. Nothing is sacred in your pursuit of excellence!"

A proven strategy for effective organization is *evaluation*.

to implement successfully. But, without these moves your team may not reach the potential it was intended to realize.

"You have to be willing to change your habits if you want to change your results."

Maybe it's time to sit down and take a long, hard look at what you have been doing to avoid the decline of your success. Maybe it's time to ask the

question out loud that everyone is thinking. Maybe it's time to take a step in a
new direction.

Just one step. One small shift that can make a huge impact.
We call this the ONE DEGREE SHIFT.

As you head down your road of success, we all should know that 180 degree
shifts can be seriously disrupting. Even 45 or 20 degree shifts can seem like a
Mt. Everest climb.

In perspective, a simple change, a small change that moves the direction just
one degree is easier to start, and sustain. In reality, a one degree shift
sustained over time is a major difference in outcome.

Try it in your car driving down the highway sometime. Move the wheel just
one small degree to the left and see how long it takes to end up in another
lane.

Small changes can make a big difference.
Time to *evaluate*.

**"You may explore, you may evaluate but you can't execute if you are not
willing to take action. Decide to take off now!"**

Israelmore Ayivor
How the Best Teams Win

3

reorganization

Now that you have your sights set on your *destination*, and have paused to
make your *evaluation*, the journey really begins. Take a deep look at what
you have, who you have and where you are headed.

This is critical.
your philosophical plan to make things better.

It takes guts to pull out your ax and begin cutting with realism. But, it must be done if you are to grow and succeed as a team.

REORGANIZATION (noun): *ensuring the right people are in the right places to make the right things happen.*

To be successful, the reorganization must improve
Keys to an effective *reorganization*:

1. Use a positive motto

To sell the change, you need a great motto people can get behind and support. When John F. Kennedy was running for President he constantly harped on the staid administration of the current President, Dwight Eisenhower, by stating, "Let's get this country moving again!" It resonated with the voters and helped Kennedy turn things around and win the election.

2. State your new destination clearly

A famous general once said, "Don't give orders your troops can understand, give orders they cannot possibly misunderstand!"

This is critical. When you are moving people away from what has always been done, make certain they have no doubt where the new organization is heading, and why.

3. Move with the movers

people. Since you have a chance to reorganize, make sure you rebuild it right. You are not obligated to keep the same people in their same positions. Now is the time to strengthen your team leadership.

To paraphrase Jim Collins from his book *Good to Great*, get the right people on the bus, and put them in the right seats on the bus.

"Executives owe it to the organization and to their fellow workers *not* to tolerate nonperforming individuals in important jobs."

Peter Drucker
The leadership and members of the team need to

what roles.

4. Eliminate programs and methodologies that are not working

The two most important elements of
reorganization are *cutting waste* and *increasing results*. There is no better time to change the details of the old plan than at the point of establishing the new one. Reset your foundation by streamlining your previous bulky ways of doing business that had wasted your time and resources.

It is time to to make some tough choices to set a new direction.
5. Be innovative and take risks You have crossed the Rubicon and now you are committed to a new way of functioning. The
play. It is a new day for your team. It's time to grow, go for it!
"Why do anything unless it is going to be great?"
Peter Block

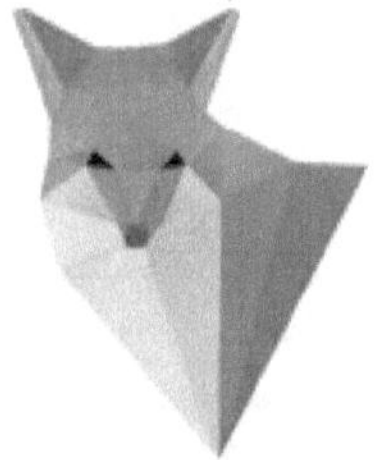

"An organization's ability to learn, and translate that learning into action rapidly, is the ultimate competitive advantage."

Jack Welch
I have a good friend who was asked by his pastor to

my friend did was evaluate or review all of the programs, leadership and strengths of the young people in both the senior and junior high departments.

Then, he challenged the way they were doing things and the kids and sponsors themselves. He was not surprised by the results of his exhortation to them. Most of the senior high students left the church because the new programs were going to tax them from a spiritual and popularity aspect with their friends.

The volunteer youth leader was left with 10 senior high kids and about 20 junior highers. Even both sets of adult sponsors bowed out. So, he recruited ten college students to replace the older sponsors and put them in leadership on a volunteer basis.

Then, he weeded out the group and divided the leaders from the followers and moved with the movers. Three other churches in the area liked what he was doing and they asked him to include their youth groups in his program, as well.

He lined up seven public schools who gave him a room after school for his ministry meetings and within one year, his little group of 30 kids had grown to over 1,000 students involved in meetings every week.

It became the largest youth ministry in California at that time, simply by following the principles outlined in this book, beginning with *reorganization*. Was it a miracle?

On some level, sure. But more than that, it was sound business sense and solid execution along with implementation of the truths needed to *change* an organization for the better.

"Quality is the result of a carefully constructed cultural environment. It has to be the fabric of the organization, not part of the fabric."

Phil Crosby

Fast forward to a more recent team that struggled and was starving for a win.

Tom Ricketts purchased the Chicago Cubs organization in 2009. His *destination* was to win the World Series. The impetus of his reorganization was to hire Theo Epstein as his new president of baseball operations in 2011.

As moves are made to bring in experienced talent and

to be done.

Players are released and literally in 4 years the roster has been greatly improved. Then, Joe Maddon is hired as the the new skipper for the Cubs in 2014.

Notice the time frame. Reorganization doesn't happen over night. It is a process that takes time.
Maddon continues the *reorganization* process as he
order and more.

manager worked together to reorganize the team on their journey to win the Division in 2015, and then the World Series in 2016.

A 108 year drought from winning it all was gone, just like that!
Well, not so fast.

The *win* was the end, it was the visual result of a set destination. It happened, though, because of many other factors, including *reorganization*.

Make sure that as you set your sights on your vision and goals you don't jump to measurement of results. Make sure you have the right people and resources included to accomplish your goal.

You and your team need to work the strategies outlined here on your journey toward winning the next season and creating your dynasty.

I'll give you this truth, not every person or team will change as much as the Cubs did on their journey. Let's be clear: no organization will grow and sustain success without embracing the occasional *reorganization* and shift in focus and strategy.
Staying the same will give you the same results.

You want higher, broader, and lasting results because you are an achiever. So, don't be afraid; rather, be critical of where you are and be open to new ways to your victorious horizon.

It is critical that the *reorganization* that follows is true to the philosophy that dictates the successful changes.

**" The distance between
number one and number two is always a constant.**

**If you want to improve the organization, you have to improve yourself
and the organization
gets pulled up with you."**

Indra Nooyi
How the Best Teams Win

4

administration

Administration is the primary job of the leader of people (remember,
everyone is a leader).
ADMINISTRATION (noun): *the ability to effectively execute activities related to
guiding a team to victory.* There are a variety of administrators, most of them

The ideal administrative leader is a powerful blend of both styles. That type
of person is a special individual, one we should all strive to become. Teams
with that blended talent have the luxury of achieving results while

In other words, the people on your team achieve success and have fun doing
it! Who wouldn't want some of that?

**"In this ever-changing society, the most powerful and enduring brands
are built from the heart.**

They are real and sustainable. Their foundations are stronger because they are built with the strength of the human spirit, not an ad campaign. The companies that are lasting are those that are authentic."

Although this book is more about the team than the leader, we need leaders in every team. And, don't miss this, you can lead from any chair!

Let's discuss the most important assets of an effective administrator:
1. Decisiveness

washy may be the hallmark of a parent who spoils his child, but when it comes to corporate leadership there is only one way to steer the ship presidents and employees need to know that someone is in charge. Make a decision, good or bad, but demonstrate conviction in the manner of moving forward.

2. Delegates to others

The greatest leaders I have worked for all had this asset in common. They knew how to make heroes out of those they managed. This is critical for a leader, not to take the credit or control everything around them, but to step back and encourage the greatness in others. (See chapter 5 for more on this topic.)

3. Grace under pressure This is the gift shared by many leaders in times

Lincoln, FDR, Reagan, Meir, Thatcher, Corazon and Aguino, who faced World Wars, strife, criticism, and depressed economies. Nothing fazed these men and women who stood tall at the lowest moments in their nations' history.

Leadership is not a roller coaster, it is a Rock of Gibraltar.

**"When written in Chinese, the word *crisis* is composed of two characters. One represents danger and
the other represents opportunity."**

John F. Kennedy

4. Innovative A great administrator is willing to deviate, to

company to change for the better. He or she takes risks realizing that the worst corporate problem is stagnation. If the company is going down, it will go down creatively, not because of inattention or by playing it safe. (See chapter 8 for more on this topic.)

5. Ethical

As the leader, the administrator has all the character tools to steer his people to greatness, personal responsibility, honesty, integrity and the courage to always do the *right* thing. This is so true, and so needed in our world today. I'm proud of the book we published, A *Leader Worth Following*, which is focused on this incredibly important asset.
This person worth following, is a powerful force for good that propels the team to the destination.

always for the team, for the common goal, for what is right and for a legacy of good.

6. Humble

The human ego can be a great asset if managed correctly and a fatal detriment if not. It is always good to remember that the ability to admit a mistake, as a leader and teammate, can be the success or failure of not just the Administrator but the entire team as well.

True story:

During the Civil War, Colonel Charles Scott, lost his wife. He was denied his request for leave to attend the funeral and comfort his children. Scott worked the chain of command until he reached President Lincoln, who met with him and responded: "Am I to have no rest? Is there no hour when I may escape these constant requests? Why do you follow me here with such business as this?...you ought to remember that I have other duties to attend to—heaven knows, enough for one man... I have all the burdens I can carry."

Early the next morning Scott heard a knock at his door. Upon opening it, he sees the president. Lincoln took Scott's hands, held them, and broke out: "My dear colonel, I was a brute last night. I have no excuse to offer. I was weary to the last extent, but I had no right to treat a man with rudeness who has offered his life to his

a regretful night and now come to beg your forgiveness." This apology served to deepen Scott's loyalty to Lincoln and his vision.

There is power in an apology. It builds credibility, respect and loyalty. Admitting you're wrong should not be viewed as weakness. On the contrary, it shows humility and deference to others, fostering a stronger relationship to you, and building a bond of trust.

It is not a shame to fall, but it is a travesty not to learn from the fall and rise again to make it right.
**"A man must be big enough to admit his mistakes,
and strong enough to correct them."**
John C. Maxwell

Always remember that. In summary, an active and strong *administration*, based on the above qualities, will affect the success of the team.

Whatever role you play on the team, these attributes can be lived out. Regardless of your age, your background, your position, your education or your location, *you* can ensure the key elements of *administration* are alive and well in your team.

How the Best Teams Win

5

delegation

company that supplied newsprint to publications. For
pay its way.

One day, Getz was confronted in a meeting by one of his vice presidents who
was frustrated with his boss's inability to okay a minor project the company
had to complete with a media outlet.

When he walked in and sat down he noticed Getz
minutes, he sat silently waiting for their meeting to begin
paper in his copy machine, and called a local restaurant to make dinner
reservations for he and his wife that night.

The junior executive was dumbfounded. He asked his CEO, "Don't you have
an assistant or someone else on our team who can do all of those things?"

Getz looked at him. Stunned. It hit him.

He had been struggling. He was always stressed and under pressure, never
having enough time for the most important work. He never had the time or
bandwidth to strategize or dream.

And the team was struggling too. Everyone was in chaos. Each day at 3PM
simple daily tasks. Getz realized he brought this upon himself, and his team.

By trying to do everything, nothing was actually
standards.
For things to change, *he* had to change.

DELEGATION (noun): *the act of giving control, authority, a job, a duty to
another person, the act of empowerment for another.*

give away his or her control. If you want your team to grow beyond a single
person, that is exactly what must be done to achieve success.

Don't try and do everything yourself, because you can't."
Anthea Turner
It is human nature to resist the urge to keep control over anything, everything, and everyone.
Resist the urge to do it.

There are few things that are nobler in life than to make heroes out of others. Letting them be the shining stars just makes your galaxy brighter!

Bill Gates would have never seen Microsoft become a billion dollar company if he spent his days and months repairing computers instead of leading all of the innovations to expand his company.

Dave Thomas used to be a fry cook at Wendy's, but
dollar franchise.

Can you imagine Oprah Winfrey cleaning mirrors and stocking bottles of waters in the green room of her show instead of *hosting* it? She was the star who knew how to delegate from her producers on down, enabling her team to become a huge success, and build an enterprise worth hundreds of millions of dollars.

Learn to delegate!

"As the leader, do the things *only* you can do, and allow others to do the rest."

Now that we are focused, let's unpack a blueprint for success when it comes to effective delegation. Your career and realizing your team's potential will depend on it.

1. Pick good people
Period.
Don't just shuttle people into empty slots, start with superstars and *create* the

slots around them.

the quality of the people you put on the team. You want success?

Start by attracting, hiring and developing the best *people*
character and chemistry for your team, you will be able to do anything.

Then train the rest.
**"In the end, all business operations can be reduced to three words,
people, product
can't do much with the other two."**
Lee Iacocca
2. Share the success

The more you let go of your ego, and let others share in your dreams and
goals, the more successful you will all become. There is power in numbers,
especially when they are multiplied over and over around you.

**"It is amazing how much people can get done if they do not worry about
who gets the credit."**
Sandra Swinney

If you enable others to succeed, you will be amazed at how your reputation
and admiration will swell up along with them. Don't hog the limelight,
broaden it. That way, more people will be part of it

Give credit away to others, doing so builds loyalty, unity and morale.
Remember our mantra: *You are better together than on your own.*
3. Guide, don't smother

If you have done a great job of choosing your quality team, back off and let
them work. They will do a good job for you. More importantly, they want to
do a good job for you. You have entrusted them to exercise their talents and
passion. They are excited that you believe in them.

In short, hold them loosely. If the people have
don't have talent and don't soar when you send them up, then go back to
number one on this list.

**"The best executive is
the one who has sense enough to pick good men to do what he wants
done, and self-restraint enough
to keep from meddling with them while they do it."**

Theodore Roosevelt

4. Make it a *perfect* Talent in one area doesn't always translate to talent in another one. Make certain your delegated

Jimmy Carter could explain all of the aspects of a nuclear submarine, but that didn't mean he could steer it. He was a highly intelligent man, maybe the smartest President since Thomas Jefferson, but not a great *leader*.

Many times, intelligence or talent does not
into the role you have assigned to him or her.
Put the people in the best position to succeed. When the team wins, everyone wins.

5. What, not how

If you want to see the maximum effect of *delegation*, focus on the ability of your delegated leaders to be themselves, not your clones. Creativity and passion are burning inside them. The best way you can bring those qualities out of them is to turn them loose and let them run with it. Then, you have truly empowered them and the future of your company.

"Never tell people how to do things. Tell them what to do and they will surprise you with their ingenuity."

General George Smith Patton, Jr.

That's *delegation*!

When I was a leader in the corporate world, I was responsible for managing a

$35 million operation, more than 150 people, and all activities and services that went along with it.

Michele was our team leader for customer service on one of our top accounts. Unfortunately, some of the response times and information coming from her team to

The client was not happy. We had an issue with an upset client and this time they were threatening to pull their business.
We needed to act fast.
Michele shared with me what was occurring, and the great news was she had ideas for a solution.
I loved them! And I believed the client would too. This was an opportunity for her to take responsibility and elevate her role as a leader.

As you probably know from me by now, I am a relationship person, so the best way I knew to handle this was face to face. Forget about emails, phone calls or a cookie care package. Our client needed to know we cared about them. They needed to hear an apology and solutions to make things right.

I will never forget the look of excitement and surprise when I asked Michele to join me for the conversation.
operations to their New York headquarters.

I took the blows from the client. I apologized for our subpar performance. I made no excuses, just agreed we failed and needed to do better. After all, I was the Plant Manager, I needed to fall on the sword.

Then came the key step: I delegated.
I turned the entire conversation over to Michele. Was I a bit nervous about what she would say? Absolutely.
Was this a key moment for us?
For sure.

Yet we had to take this step. The operation didn't run effectively because I did everything. It ran effectively because I had a great team, and I empowered them to take action. What happened?

ran with it.

"Surround yourself with

delegate authority,
and don't interfere
as long as the policy you've decided upon is being carried out."

Ronald Reagan

As she shared her solutions and strategies to improve our communication and relationship with the client, we all started to smile.

handed the baton and she did a great job. Most importantly, the client was happy. Michele came out of that meeting beaming with pride.

client. She was provided the opportunity to take the lead, and she did.

I was just as proud and pleased. I now had a leader I could trust with key decisions, communication with clients, and any future business.

We never had another issue with this client, and our business continued to grow.
It all started with one word: *delegation.*

In summary, the positive effects of delegation will ignite your organizational (and your career) success in several ways. You will:

• Forever be released from tasks others can do so you can lead

• *multiplied*
• Bring out the greatness in your team
• Realize maximum company morale
• Experience the joy of your team achieving success

• Become a leader of leaders

**"An empowered organization is one in which individuals have the knowledge, skill, desire, and opportunity
to personally succeed in a way that leads to collective organizational success."**

Stephen Covey
How the Best Teams Win

6

cooperation

You set your sights on your destination, have had a successful reorganization and learned the role of administration and the art of delegation.

Hold it! This might be the most important chapter in the book.

During every one of my presentations, I ask the attendees to list four words that come to mind as critical to the success of a team.

In every single event, in every city, town, conference and organization I visit there is one word that pops up every time.

Every time!
Cooperation.
COOPERATION (NOUN): *the process of working together to the same end.*

Simply put, if you are unable to get people to work together there will be no greatness. You will not reach your destination and there will be no organization.

Cooperation is not just an admirable concept, it is the determining lifeblood of every team rise or fall. Success is not fundamentally about dollars and cents, it's all about *relationships*.

"Teamwork makes the dream work."

Bang Gae

Believe it. People make up your teams and if they are all getting along, you have an excellent chance of winning.

If not, the lack of cooperation within your ranks will sink you as surely as the Titanic. The lack of teamwork is the iceberg lurking out there to bring you down.

**"The most powerful force ever known on this planet is human cooperation –
a force for construction and destruction."**

Jonathan Haidt

Houston. We have a problem. This begins one of the greatest stories of our country and the concept of cooperation.
Apollo 13.
Astronauts literally stranded in space without much, if any, power onboard their ship.
Forget the moon.
The team back home in Houston had a new mission. Bring them home.
(played by Ed Harris) gathers all the "experts" in a room. On the table are all the items the crew has on board the spacecraft.

He draws a visual on the board in the room so everyone can see where the ship currently is, where it will run out of power, and the distance they are short of earth.

Anything less than getting the team safely back home is unacceptable.
The rooms erupts.
One department personnel says it can't be done. Another says these things weren't built for this. One blaming the electrical, another on mechanical, and the

You may work in a hospital or other life and death organization. Most of us do not. I get the fact that the Apollo 13 situation is more heightened than most of our daily opportunities; just stay with me here.

The commander silences the room.
He didn't want excuses.
He didn't want blame.
He didn't want anyone saying what *can't* be done.

He wanted to know what was *possible* and what *could* be done. He encouraged the team to work together
Options. They come from intelligent people working together

problems. Options. It isn't about one idea, it is about many on your

What does it take? Exactly what it took that team.
Cooperation. Once they started to experiment and try different ideas, several key things happened:

1. They started to work as a unit on a common goal
2.
3. They brainstormed in a positive manner
4. They found out what didn't work
5. They then discovered steps that would work

Let's go back to the story.

One of the best and pinnacle moments is when the astronaut that didn't get to go on the mission is called to step in. They thought he had measles, so they left him home.

He didn't have measles, but he was more prepared to help on the ground than anyone else.
Coincidence?

ways to help them reduce power on board. People asked him to rest, his response "they don't get rest up there, I don't get rest down here."

We all know now they brought the crew safely home. How? It all came down to one word: *Cooperation.*

"Finding good players is easy. Getting them to play as a team is another story."
Casey Stengel
Here are some ways to improve your team's *cooperation*:
1. Participation

Get everyone involved to give them a stake in the team and a higher level of commitment to work together. If they view their job as a vocation rather than just a workday, they are more likely to get along with more people because they want the best for the group.

You need to engage your team.

valued and heard. Every person and role matters, so make sure there is a commitment to allow everyone to have a voice.

2. Personal demonstration

As the owner or manager, take the lead in showing a cooperative effort here. Don't just tell your employees to get along with others, *show* them by your attitude and actions.

"The texture of character is better caught than taught."
3. Create a positive environment Smile. Say hello. Ask people how they are doing,
worker, and then surprise them and buy their lunch. As a leader (and remember everyone is a leader) you can set the thermostat for the team. *awesome* in everything.

Start the day knowing it will be a *great* day. The acronym **G.R.E.A.T.** stands for Get Really Excited About Today!

4. Compliment constantly

Whenever you have a chance, let your team know how great they are. The more a person realizes their value, the more cooperative they will be. The essence of jealousy is insecurity. Do whatever you can to make your team members feel safe and secure at work.

**"A sure sign of a soul-based workplace is excitement, enthusiasm, real passion; not manufactured passion, but real involvement.
And there's very little fear."**

David Whyte
5. Be vigilant Maintaining *cooperation* and a commitment to

You have to work hard or things can unravel before you know it. If you sense an interpersonal problem among your managers or employees, bring them in for a meeting and try to straighten it out. If that doesn't work, separate them so they are not rubbing up against each other, deepening

troublemaker to salvage the spirit of *cooperation*. Yes, it is *that* important.

**"Truly human leadership protects an organization from the internal rivalries that can shatter a culture. When we have to protect ourselves from each other,
the whole organization suffers. But when trust and cooperation thrive, we pull together and the organization grows stronger as a result."**

Simon Sinek, Leaders Eat Last
The history of sports is a great displayer of *cooperation*. In the lingo of winning teams, the term "chemistry" is often used to describe the power behind the success in champions.

Chemistry is also known as *cooperation*, that
talent of their more skilled opponents. Vince Lombardi,

in bringing his players together. The 1980 U.S. Olympic hockey gold
medalists lived together for several months and truly cared about each other
before they upset the sporting world.

Every year, an underdog emerges to either win a title or make it to the
championship game because This cooperation is magical as it demonstrates a
true commitment not just to the games, but to each other.

When you build your leadership team, look for men and women of
cooperation. They will be exactly what your company needs to grow beyond
talent and technique. They will be *team players*.

"T.E.A.M. – Together Everyone Achieves More."
Unknown

It's ironic that last quote came from an unknown source, don't you think? No
one individual takes the credit for it. I like that.

Let's break that acronym down.

Together *everyone achieves more!* So it starts, simply, with a mandated
understanding that this quest to victory isn't about one person. It means
playing the game hard for the name on the front of your jersey versus the
name on the back.

*Together **everyone** achieves more!* When you focus on your team and help
others win, then everyone wins! A team leaves no one out, and victory is for
all.

*Together everyone **achieves** more!* It is good to this is about making
something happen. We need to be
souls. Execution is a must for a team to succeed.
**"Happiness lies in the joy of achievement and the thrill of creative
effort."**
Franklin D. Roosevelt
*Together everyone achieves **more**!* Remember, winning once is good.

Repeating victory is great.

"Coming together is a beginning. Keeping together is progress. Working together is success."

Henry Ford
Saying that, *cooperation* does not mean an absence

Make sure your verbal and written battlings are respectful, since you are all on the same team and want a similar result, to be the best team you can be. Here is a mantra to live by that fosters this type of cooperation:

"Harder on the issues, softer on the people."
Jim Therrien

cooperation . In fact, it needs to do exactly that for the sake of getting better so that in the end, everyone goes out and drinks a toast to the creative ideas and innovative programs that spell greatness.

Just learn to always do it together.

"Life is not a game of Solitaire; people depend on one another. When one does well, others are lifted. When one stumbles, others also are impacted. There are no one-man teams—

Success is a *cooperative* effort; it is dependent upon those who stand beside you."
Jon M. Huntsman Sr., *Essential Lessons on Leadership*

There is simply not a team if you do not find ways to have *cooperation*. Focus on keeping the main thing the main thing (the destination,) and on doing the right thing by *helping others win* and you will reap amazing rewards.

7

continuation

Continuation needs to be just as passionate as your evaluation, reorganization, cooperation and delegation, or

" *May today m*ark the beginning of many new joys and accomplishments and a*continuation* of all of the good things that you have already achieved."

Dale Nielsen

The greatest corporate example of the process from evaluation to reorganization to administration to delegation to continuation can be found in the miracle of Apple, Inc. based in Cupertino, California.

because of a power struggle with its Board of Directors. For the next ten years, the company spiraled downward. In 1996, Jobs was asked to serve as the interim CEO
A year later, he was named the permanent CEO and magic began to happen. and what he saw demanded a major reorganization for it to survive. He slashed 350 projects in development down
involved in the corporation. But, Steve Jobs knew exactly what he was doing here.
taking innovator. He followed through on his belief that the best chance for Apple's success was to go for the,

He created the iMac, iTunes, the iPod and the iPhone. Then, he changed the image of the company into a more edgy look targeting the younger, hipper crowd.

He brought in young executives and delegated, giving them the freedom to create from their own talent, ingenuity and passion.

Steve Jobs kept the pressure on with a daily continuation of what they had laid down in corporate stone here. He pounded the market place with his new products and the results were astounding.
success story of the Century.

only in constant improvement and constant change."
Tom Peters

Continuation is not glamorous but it is practical and gritty enough to keep your team from slipping back into the rusting of eroding complacency that leads to frustration and destruction.

Like a powerful football team or a healthy

company way of life. When a team is in a , leaders can feel it, employees can feel it and even those you serve can sense it.

making and optimism that accompanies the feeling of why everything is working together. The dread, that had preceded the evaluation needed to save the status quo, is long gone, replaced now by a plan of action and a renewed spirit of success.

That's exactly what Steve Jobs accomplished when he got Apple back on track. He not only cut out the unnecessary costs, he stabilized the company and got it working again.

exploded in the pockets of everyone who owned them. That is *continuation*. A company that surpasses itself in excellence every day and as a result reaps the rewards
"Average corporations compete with others. Great corporations compete with themselves."
W. Southwick
maintaining your direction. **The importance of *continuation*:**

1. Keeps your reorganization on track First and foremost, continuation keeps your reorganization moving forward with the same

all that hard work to evaluate and change your company you want to make certain what happens after that is successful.

**"Practice the philosophy
of continuous improvement. Get a little bit better every single day.
Excellence is not a destination; it is a *continuous* journey that never
ends."**

Brian Tracy

2. Keeps morale up Reorganization is always scary and when you follow it up with a successful continuation series,
morale within a team is more than important, it is *vital*.

3. Allows more risk-taking

With a successful running operation and a strong foundation established by your continuation programs, you now have the luxury to experiment and implement new ideas and programs that can

Why? You are the front runner now.

You are not desperate and searching for answers, rather, you are focused and stand an excellent chance at even more success.

4. Prevents complacency and stagnation

"Keep moving forward, keep moving forward, keep moving forward." This is a quote that reminds you that you are on the right track, and a very *powerful* one. There is no longer the possibility of complacency or stagnation as long as you are moving ahead.

"No company can afford *not* to move forward.

It may be at the top of the heap today but at the bottom of the heap tomorrow, if it doesn't."

J. C. Penney

5. Keeps internal pride going

The beauty of continuation is that it promotes an ongoing spirit of excellence within the team. Everyone wants to do better than they ever have because of the success bandwagon effect created. Day in and day out, everyone wants to perform well, be better and win.

issues and verbally powerful. He was so good, in fact, that his poll numbers changed following the debate showing him leading the President.

Even worse for Obama, during the debate he was shown several times on camera pouting, angry and seemingly offended he even had to be there at the debate.

But, *continuation* is not just a concept, it is a reality, even in politics. Simply put, all the hard work Romney had

the next two confrontations. He stumbled and slogged through them and the President picked up his game and pounded Romney like a wrecking ball on balsa wood.

Romney lost his edge and as a result, lost the election. He never became president because he failed to demonstrate continuous excellence despite his opening coup.

Remember, it's not where you start, it's where you *continuation*. It takes all of your hard work, and in the end, rewards you.

When you have your opportunity, don't let up. Why give away all your insightful evaluation, cohesive reorganization, dynamic destination, quality delegation, just to fall short during the ongoing maintenance of them and lose in the end?

A lesson Mitt Romney learned all too painfully. Continuation involves quality control, consistency, daily passion and a persistence that matches the glory
Don't let up now.

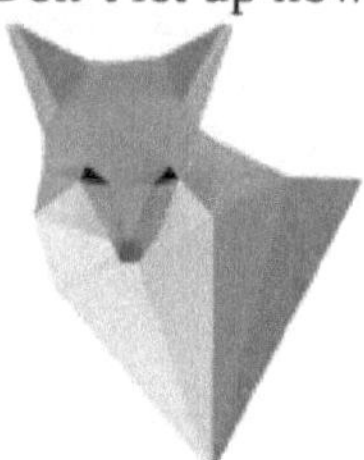

"If you stop learning, you stop creating history...and become history."
Vadim Kotelnikov

Through over two decades of my career in the game of basketball, I have been fortunate to referee over 1,000 games. I've seen amazing teams.

Half of them have lost.
The other half...you guessed it...have won. And some of them won repeatedly.
Why do those same teams keep on winning? They never quit, they never give up, they never stop

Let's highlight one example.

Team A is winning the basketball game by more than 30 points with just two minutes left in the game. The coach continues to shout out plays and even calls for the players to continue strong full court defensive pressure on the "soon to be losing team."

Why?
Continuation.

Some people get up and leave the game, or stop competing. Some fans complain that they are "rubbing it in." What those people don't understand is the concept of *continuation*.

A competitor never quits, it just isn't in them.

The coach knows that habits repeated will become habits formed. Even though *that* game may be decided, the importance of good habits remains.

There will be another game, another day, another time to face problems and the need to perform at a high level.

Additionally, in games that have large point spreads both teams give experience to players that rarely get in the action.

So, *everyone* keeps the pressure on.
working hard, keep making good decisions, keep doing the right th*ings..and never* give up!

This type of work ethic is what continuation is all about. This drive is what makes champions, well, champions. The constant desire to do your best, to work with excellence and never get tired of improving.

Teams that stop will eventually lose.
Teams that continue will win.

Never stop. Never consider one basket a winning game. Never take one victory and call it a winning season. Never stop after one winning season on the ques*t for repeat*ed success.

Heck no!
You're after a dynasty!
Continuation is not glamorous. It's routine, often dull,

may erode in quality and ability to achieve results. You cannot take your eye off the road here or you will crash and burn.

Stay the course in a consistent and attentive manner. You and your team will be glad you did.
As Winston Churchill once said,

**"Every day you may make progress. Every step may be fruitful.
Yet there will stretch out before you
an ever-lengthening, ever-ascending, ever-improving path.
You know you will never get to the end of the journey."**

How the Best Teams Win

8

innovation

We have all heard the famous phrase, "grow or die." Start growing now.

Figure out what needs to be changed and take some creative risks.

With your organization running strongly the time is ripe for new ideas and programs. You can afford to take calculated risks now because you have a healthy margin for error.

INNOVATION (noun): *the act or process of introducing new ideas or methods.*

a football game when you have a three touchdown lead. A coach in that position doesn't need a desperation Hail Mary pass because his team is ahead and doing well.

Now is the time to mix it up, vary the offense, because the defense is expecting you to sit on your lead and be predictable by running the ball up the middle on almost every play.

**"When your company is rolling along smoothly and you have the money to burn that is the perfect time for innovation, not when you're struggling
but when you're strong."**

Bob Bailey
evaluation of how to save it.

He eliminated several products that were costing money but not selling. Then, he streamlined the customer care process, added two new managers and rebuilt his employee team. Within six months, the company began

After enjoying a reliable continuation and the solid foundation it now afforded him to take some risks, David decided it was time for some innovations. He sat down with his managers and suggested,

furniture and computers. Plus, I want us to do discount promotions like we have never done before. It is time to accelerate our brand."

unthinkable only months before, were a rousing success. They followed a winning formula and within a year, David opened two new stores in the city. The *innovation* made that possible.

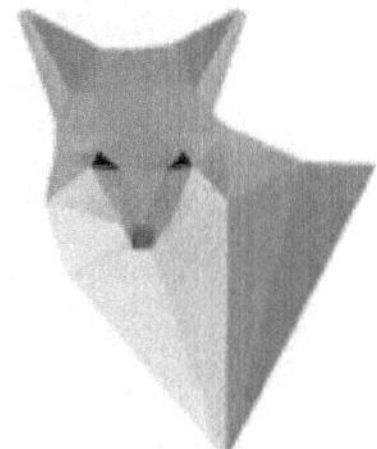

"The heart and soul of the company is creativity and innovation."
Bob Iger

It is important here to note that innovation is not just an attitude or a concept, it is a practical *application* of your creative idea. It's one thing to "paper bet" on the

money at real risk. *Innovation* is like that.

Anyone can talk a good game, but the true world innovators follow through and make their dreams a reality. They are not afraid to step out and make changes. They are not afraid of failure.

What are the keys to becoming a successful *innovator*?
1. Dare to Dream

Get out outside the "corporate box." It is a trap to always play it safe and never venture from it. Remember this powerful adage from a brilliant man:

"If you always do what you always did, you'll always get what you always got."
Albert Einstein
Dare to dream…yep.
2. Build your foundation If you have a solid base to work from, it is not

Always work from a position of strength instead of a place of weakness. The time to double your bet in a poker game is when you are awash in chips, not when you are down to a few.

3. Before you add *innovation* to your organization, do your homework. Talk to specialists in the

give you the pros and cons of what to expect. It is *innovation* not ignoration. You do not need to be the expert but you need the expertise.

4. Take the Step

This is the hardest part of *innovation*…actually implementing it. Anyone can talk a good game, but it is the truly brilliant leaders who will put one foot forward and *do* it. I cannot stress this enough, *innovation* is not creativity, *it is the practical application of it.*

"A.C.T. Action Changes Things"
Unknown
5. Complacency is limited success

As wonderful as continuation is, it has walls governing it. It can only go so far towards your ultimate goals. *Innovation* is part of continuity. It is that part of your journey with wings.

You cannot innovate from Los Angeles to New York. You can only make it your goal to get there and map out your new ideas and changes with stops along the way. But, at some point you may

Be willing to take to the air when you need to.

"Success breeds complacency. Complacency breeds failure."

Andy Grove

Enjoy your continuation, but never be lulled to sleep by it.

The Wright Brothers were enamored by a great invention called the bicycle. They evaluated it, reorganized it and soon were completing all the steps to building a dynamic foundation for an even greater mode of transportation based on their work and creativity with

They had built a solid continuation both

bicycle shop to another level. It was called the *airplane.* Talk about stepping outside the box!

The Wright Cycle Exchange company opened in 1892. By 1903, they were standing on the shores of Kitty Hawk, North Carolina, about to launch air travel.

Without the money earned and all the evaluation and reorg from their initial endeavors, there would not *Innovation* has to have a foundation. In this case, it had a great one.

"Dreamers are mocked as impractical. The truth is they are the most practical, as their innovations lead to progress and a better way of life for all of us."

Robin S. Sharma

Innovation is challenging, especially when you are attempting to sustain a winning a team. Knowing when to take risks for improvement is important. Here are some guidelines to use as you implement your creativity:

•
• Make your move out of logic, not emotion
• Verify any risk with experienced counsel in areas

• Be prepared to live with the consequences if your innovation fails
• If you can, take risks *gradually*

• Be open to modify or alter your innovation process as you go along
• If you hear your inner voice constantly telling you to back off, postpone…
listen!

Many great organizations are successful in sustaining success as a team through *innovation*, notably, Disney. After establishing Disneyland in July 1955, there was plenty of money at the core to branch out into movies. *Old Yeller, The Shaggy Dog, Pollyanna* and *The Parent Trap* followed.

The same year that Disneyland opened, Walt Disney came with an inexpensively produced television show for kids, , which became one of the

too. Who hasn't seen, *Lady and the Tramp, Cinderella, Pinocchio* and *Bambi?*

to take advantage of color television. *Walt Disney's Wonderful World of Color* debuted on NBC, the pioneer in that trendy genre.

In 1971, Disney corporation opened their second amusement park, *Walt Disney World* and eleven years later, *EPCOT* was born.

Another big innovation, beyond just being *on* TV, Disney moved to cable, with their own network, the Disney Channel, in 1985. Then it was off to Broadway in 1994, as Disney took the huge smash movie *Beauty and Beast*

In more recent years, Disney ventured into digital animation with Pixar, into major iconic series brands with Marvel and Star Wars, and the list goes on and on.

Space does not permit us to list all of the *innovations* that Disney Entertainment has brought into the world

innovation was a healthy blend of
meet a need; but it was always followed by action.

**"We keep moving forward, opening new doors, and doing new things,
because we're curious and curiosity keeps leading us down new paths."**

Walt Disney

If you want a blueprint on how a team can innovate, how and when, just
study the Disney model. They never lost their position of economic strength,
while adding

entertainment is legendary.

Innovation
up your future as well. Any new product, sales technique, idea, process or
marketing method is exciting to people and it can ignite much needed energy.

The process of change is not just about the content, but the timing as well.
Always remember that truth. If you do, you will be see amazing results
because of your innovative leadership!

**"There is no progress without risk, and in an environment where change
is accelerating, risks are multiplying and businesses are increasingly
complex… companies need strong, innovative partners to help manage
their risk."**

Mike McGavick
How the Best Teams Win

motivation

The ability for you, your team members, and your leadership to stay motivated is paramount to your success. Every strategy in *game plan* hinges on whether or not you are committed to making it happen.

as this is the moment we cannot forget. It is too critical. We need to remind ourselves of the game plan. It begins with a drive toward your destination with courage to take action in your reorganization. A

for effective cooperation. The leadership is grounded in humility through constant evaluation, and cements relationships with trust in continuation, and always grows with wise innovation.

Wow! What an amazing plan.
As long as you have the *motivation* to see each step through, with excellence.

"Desire is the key to motivation, but it's determination and commitment to an unrelenting pursuit of your goal –

a commitment to excellence – that will enable you to attain the success you seek."

Mario Andretti
This isn't just *a mi*nd game. This is something we
team members inspired, committed, dedicated to the cause.

Every day you have a choice to make.
All in!
Or not.
I know you are all in, so let's bring this home!

Try these ideas to keep the passion and stay in your motivation mode:
1. Have a personal success shelf

People need encouragement. We need to know that the value we bring, the work we do, matters. It fuels us.

Remember back to when you were young; perhaps you played little league, or were in scouts, or participated in band, debate club, something where you did good work and were given something for that work. In most communities, the winners received ribbons, trophies, medals and such (unlike today, but that is another book). If you were like me, you put them on a shelf.

Do that today! Maybe it isn't a literal shelf, but it's something you can look at to celebrate everyday accomplishments. Have daily tasks and check them off. Even if they are small, you feel a sense of accomplishment, worth, which fuels you for tomorrow.

You need to remind yourself of victories, big and small. Every victory matters.

2. Celebrate people

The same as above holds true for everyone on your team. People crave someone saying, "nice job!" We don't say "thank you" enough, we don't appreciate enough, we just don't.
Take this great idea from a true story.

All of the staff gathered for the quarterly Most Valuable Player announcement. Kimberly was excited, honored, and a bit humbled when her name was called,

as she walked to the front of the room, shook hands with

It wasn't typical for her to brag, but she was proud of the work she had done, and from her emotional response, it was obvious to everyone how moved she was to be recognized by her peers.

That's right!

This program was for nominations by any of the staff; where anyone could be nominated, by anyone. It was for outstanding work, for helping a coworker or client, by going above and beyond.

All of the employees showed up for this traditional quarterly event, to applaud their peers and to see if they might be among the chosen few for the honor of being a Most Valuable Player!

praise publicly raises the impact. The accolades can motivate them to continue to perform at high levels, and challenges everyone to raise their performance levels. What can you do in your team to create such a powerful program?

Remember, action changes things.
3. Have the right mental approach

How you approach each day, each project, each moment will have a direct impact on your success rate. A poor attitude demotivates. A positive, upbeat attitude enhances our *motivation*.

It's going to be a G.R.E.A.T. day!
You need to believe it and repeat it, *every day.*

"People often say that motivation doesn't last. Well, neither does bathing —

that's why we recommend it daily."

Zig Ziglar

How's your attitude? Think about it, really think about it.

Are you someone others want to be around? Someone that can bring the best out of the team? A person that doesn't see the glass as half full, Simply put:

"The altitude of your success is in direct relationship to your attitude in life."
4. Believe in your team

Nothing powers the vehicle of *motivation* inside a person like knowing they are trusted. Empowering people to do great work is akin to a

Light them up and watch them soar!

There are so many steps you can take to show team members you trust them, believe in them and care for them.

Let's highlight this concept of *motivation* through another true story: Rebecca, the new CEO, addressed the leaders at her team was ready to beat the competition and exceed goals.

As she passed out cards to her 200 leaders, Rebecca stated, "For us to succeed this year, we need to take care of our customers at the highest level. We can't let in fear of failure, nor rest on past practices, nor lose any inspiration to be great. We need to be creative and do what is needed to service them. Each of you has a 'get out of jail free – we believe in you' card. It's like a 'get out of jail free' card, but built on trust, and I want you to use it.

Take action this year without asking permission. We believe in you, we trust you."

A few months later, Lisa used her card. The product for her clients' event was not done in time to make the overnight shipment. Lisa had to take action, she knew her leadership was behind her. She chartered a plane and

This "wow" moment created a very loyal client. The moment was inspired because leadership supported her actions, and that *motivation* allowed her talent to be shown.

There is power in empowerment, literally.
You have an opportunity with your team, to expand their horizons and take positive action that gets results.

People that empower their teams encourage talented people to be their best. You need to *wow* your team by showing them you trust them, so they can *wow* you with their best.

5. Have some pride to reach your destination
You simply have to *want it!*

Bottom line, failure does happen, but you aren't a failure until you quit. And I know you aren't a quitter.

Dig deep. Get out of bed each day prepared to take on the world.

**"Wanting something is not enough. You must hunger for it.
Your motivation must be absolutely compelling in order to overcome the obstacles that will invariably come your way."**

Les Brown
One of my best friends is a husband, father and a great man. His name is Jeff Cross.
Jeff has the wonderful privilege of making a living

Many people see Jeff and admire his life, what he does and seem to want the rewards of his life; but few are willing to give what he gave.

Through years of professional development training from the best in the business, to individual critique via
all.

Oh, he had challenges and failure, and you will have them too. There are so many hurdles that we don't know are present until we run into them. You may even fall down.

So what.
Get back up. Jeff did.
It is about your *motivation* to reach your *destination.*

nation. Each night, that team is set up as a subset group of 3 people, with a goal to have a great game. Each game leads to the next game, and ultimately to the next season.

Not much different than your team.
Early in Jeff's game plan journey, he had a night to remember, or forget.
He and his team, the crew of 3, were working the game, and all was good, until…
To protect the innocent, we will change the names of the infamous crew of three to Larry, Moe and Curly.

Larry makes a foul call on a shot attempt. Moe walks past Larry and tells him "the ball went in." Naturally, Larry is appreciative of the information and trusts his teammate, so he reports the foul and counts the basket. The place erupts! The coach goes nuts.

Larry is shell shocked.

In a panic he quickly runs over to Curly, trying to hide his head in the sand like an ostrich. "Curly, did you see the ball go in?"

Curly simply says, "What ball?"

Oh my, what a response! What ball? The basketball, knucklehead. Ever feel that way about a teammate, or even yourself?

Larry is beside himself and turns to Moe, and with a bit more frustration and expectation, "Moe, are you *sure* that ball went in?"

"Not anymore!" claims Moe.
So, the crew isn't sure what to do, they leave the call as is. They count the basket.
Of course, the game goes into overtime and the team they awarded those 2 points to, wins the game… And they shouldn't have.
empted by a phone call from the conference coordinator,
Not only was an error made, but their inaccurate ruling changed the outcome of the game, ouch! You've been there, and you may be there again.

This is where pride, determination, persistence, and *motivation* to reach your destination, will rise up and help you win, or alternatively, sink you and your team to depths where you can no longer breathe.

learn, to keep going. Motivation won out, and years later, so did he.
happen. He fought for it. He used that moment to get better, to believe he could do it. It was fuel to move upward. Simply put, it was in his game plan. And for the rest of the crew that night too. His partners from that memorable night have gone on to
All for the sake of their teammates, the game and the
This quote sums it up,
is when the game is over and everyone forgets they were there."
Unknown

Being a part of a team is a wonderful treat. It is the highest honor when victory happens and we are privileged to be on stage with other talented, passionate, dedicated men and women.

You are better together than you are on your own. Downturns are easier to recover from with the help of a team. Success is sweeter when enjoyed with others.

There is no doubt, you go further and faster together, but only when everyone plays their part with excellence. Time to soar. Time to take your team to your destination!
You can achieve amazing and wonderful dreams, goals and results; if you consistently go for them.

Your team can make this their best year ever, together, as long as your collective motivation is to do whatever it takes to make it. And to do it for one another.

The world can be transformed and a better place because you were here, if only you choose to do something with what you're given.

Commit to being a great employee and team member, every day, in every moment and on every task.
Commit to being a great spouse, friend, parent, child, sibling and friend,

every day, every conversation. Commit to improving your community as a
neighbor, volunteer, and citizen.
In other words, *get some motivation!*

**"If you believe in yourself, have dedication and pride – and never quit,
you'll be a winner. The price of victory is high but so are the rewards."**

Paul Bryant
This is really a heart issue. You simply have to stay the course. Keep running
until the race is over. Keep
eloquently said, "it ain't over 'til it's over."
Believe! Never give up on *your* game plan! *How the Best Teams Win*

epilogue

This book may be coming to a close, but your journey continues.
Time to prepare for the next event, the next season, your next victory.
Your game plan is about achieving greatness and sustaining success.
Together.

Destination...evaluation...reorganization...administra tion...delegation…
cooperation…continuation…innovation.. motivation…the key *–ions* that can
turn your team, your workplace and your career into your dream come true.

That, my friends, is how you take a *game plan* and create a dynasty, a legacy,
an ongoing success.
As a leader, (remember we are all leaders because we

prepare your heart, hone your courage and seek your counsel. No matter what
happens, implement the vital steps we have discussed which will make the
difference from failure to success. Even great success.

As a child, we learned the ABCs and those basics taught us how to speak,
reason, and communicate wondrous things.

Now, as an adult leader, we need to practice similar fundamentals to never
allow the stagnation of the status quo govern us. Especially, when we know
and understand the power that lies beyond it.

You were not placed on this earth to play it safe. You are a leader and a powerful member of teams. You are one who moves people, programs and events. You have your future in *your* hands.

Hopefully, this book has helped you take your passion for success a step further and develop your *game plan!* Realize that the end of this book is just another part of a never ending cycle for your success.

The next game is around the corner. You need to either continue the plan, reorganize the plan, evaluate the plan or make innovations to the plan. And all that work needs to be done with excellent communication, a trusted sense of cooperation and unity by your team to achieve the results!

Remember: *you are better together than you are on your own.*

How much better? That is up to you. How far and wide can your success be? T. S. Eliot says it best:
"Only those who will risk going too far
Now, go out and be a great team. Work hard, play hard, and enjoy the game of life!
As always, never forget, *the world is waiting for you!*
God bless you in this and the coming years.

notes

____

____

notes

notes

www.ingramcontent.com/pod-product-compliance
Lightning Source LLC
Chambersburg PA
CBHW051501140726
47987CB00006B/2818